alphabet

Photography
George Siede and Donna Preis

Louis Weber, C.E.O.
Publications International, Ltd.
7373 North Cicero Avenue
Lincolnwood, Illinois 60646

ISBN 0–7853–1278–1

Publications Internationa

D1307653

Aa

apple

bunny

Bb

Cc

clown

Dd

duck

Ee

eggs

frog

Ff

Gg   Hh

hat

glasses

ice cream

Jj

jacket

Kk

kittens

Ll

lightbulb

mittens

Mm

Nn

net

Oo

orange

puzzle

Pp

Qq

quilt

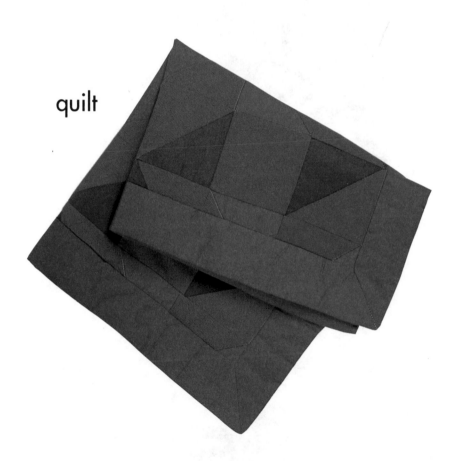

Rr

raccoon

seashells

Ss

Tt

train

umbrella

Uu

Vv

violin

Ww

wagon

Xx

xylophone

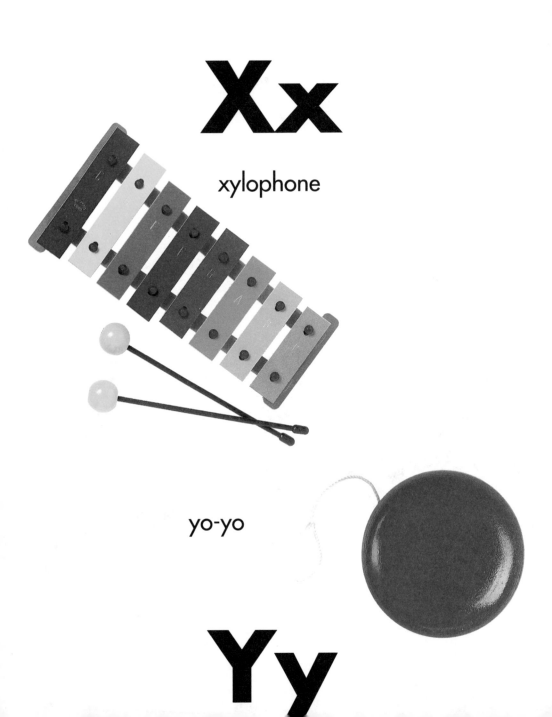

yo-yo

Yy

Zz

zippers